A Western Journal

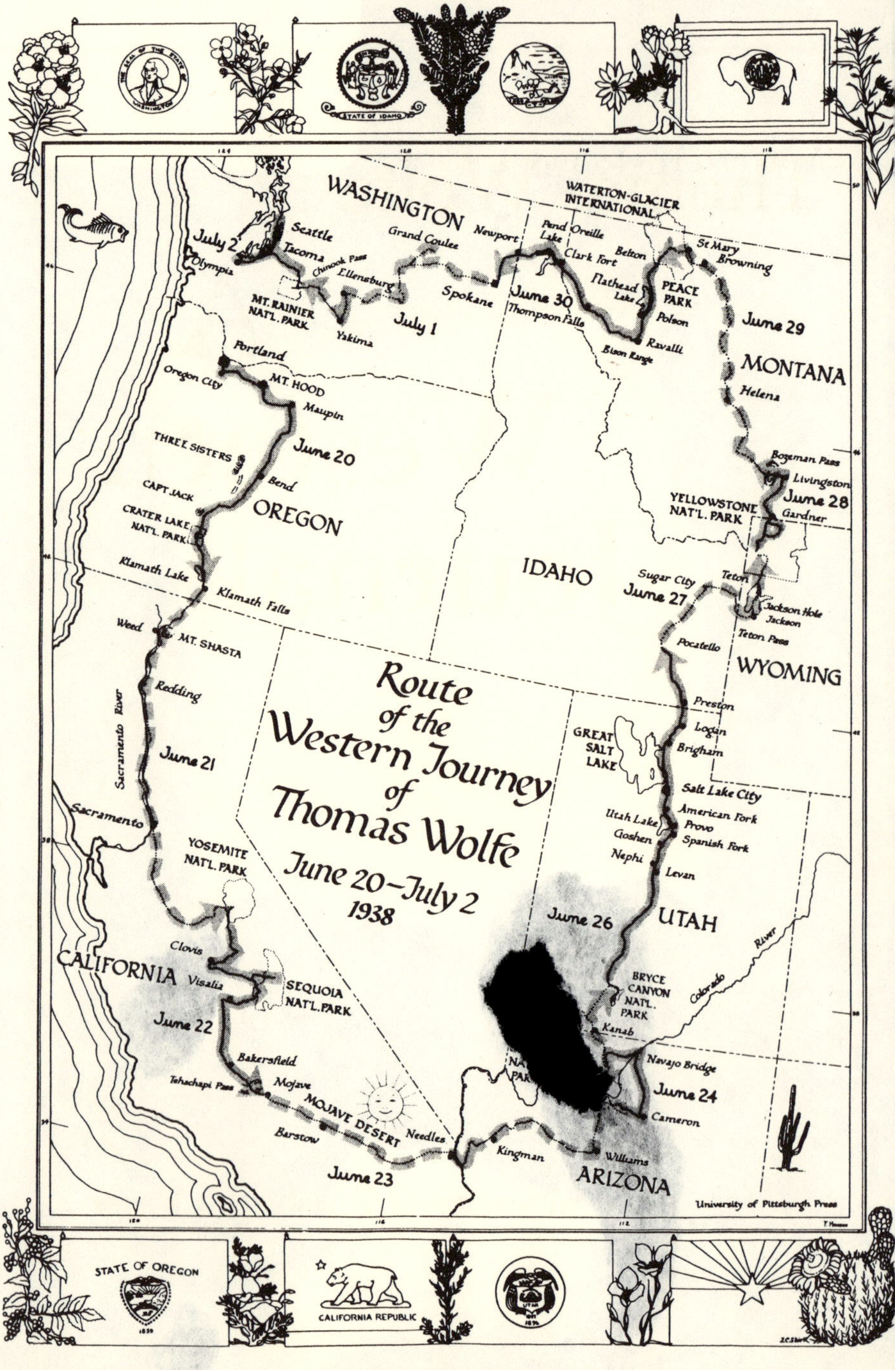

Route of the Western Journey of Thomas Wolfe
June 20–July 2
1938
WASHINGTON
OREGON
IDAHO
MONTANA
WYOMING
UTAH
CALIFORNIA
ARIZONA
WATERTON-GLACIER INTERNATIONAL
PEACE PARK
July 2
Olympia
Seattle
Tacoma
Chinook Pass
Ellensburg
Grand Coulee
Newport
MT. RAINIER NAT'L. PARK
Yakima
July 1
Spokane
Pend Oreille Lake
Clark Fork
June 30
Thompson Falls
Flathead Lake
Belton
Polson
Ravalli
Bison Range
St Mary
Browning
June 29
Helena
Bozeman Pass
Livingston
June 28
Gardner
YELLOWSTONE NAT'L. PARK
Teton
Sugar City
June 27
Jackson Hole
Jackson
Teton Pass
Pocatello
Preston
Logan
Brigham
GREAT SALT LAKE
Salt Lake City
American Fork
Provo
Spanish Fork
Utah Lake
Goshen
Nephi
Levan
June 26
BRYCE CANYON NAT'L. PARK
Kanab
Colorado River
Navajo Bridge
June 24
Cameron
Williams
Kingman
Needles
Portland
Oregon City
MT. HOOD
Maupin
June 20
THREE SISTERS
Bend
CAPT JACK
CRATER LAKE NAT'L. PARK
Klamath Lake
Klamath Falls
Weed
MT. SHASTA
Redding
Sacramento River
June 21
Sacramento
YOSEMITE NAT'L. PARK
Clovis
Visalia
SEQUOIA NAT'L. PARK
June 22
Bakersfield
Tehachapi Pass
Mojave
MOJAVE DESERT
Barstow
June 23
University of Pittsburgh Press
STATE OF IDAHO
STATE OF OREGON
1859
CALIFORNIA REPUBLIC
UTAH
1896

Thomas Wolfe, 1900-1938

A Western Journal

A Daily Log of the Great Parks Trip
June 20—July 2, 1938

University of Pittsburgh Press

Published by the University of Pittsburgh Press, Pittsburgh, Pa., 15260

Feffer and Simons, Inc., London
Manufactured in the United States of America

Library of Congress Catalog Card Number 51-5285
ISBN 0-8229-5121-5
Fourth Printing 1980

Note on "A Western Journey"

When Thomas Wolfe went to the Pacific Northwest in the early summer of 1938, he was impelled by a combination of strong motives. He had just delivered to his publishers a manuscript of twelve hundred thousand words. He was tired and wanted a rest. The Pacific Northwest was the only part of the United States he had never visited. Finally, he had never lost his small boy's sense of wonder and he wanted to ride on a streamlined train.

When he arrived in Portland, Oregon, he met two newspaper men who were planning a trip by automobile through all the National Parks of the Far West. They invited Wolfe, who could not drive a car himself, to go with them. He was always avid to learn all he could about his America, and he could get as drunk on new geography as on strong liquor. So, his great weariness momentarily forgotten, he accompanied his two new friends.

On July 4, 1938, the trip was over and Wolfe was in Seattle. On that day he wrote me a letter in which, for the first and only time, he spoke of "A Western Journey":

I am feeling much better already, although I have traveled ten thousand miles, five thousand in the last two weeks, and seen hundreds of new places and people. My fingers are itching to write again. I have already made fifty thousand words of notes on this journey. I propose to stay here a couple of weeks longer and get these notes revised, rounded out, and typed in a more complete form. The whole record I am calling simply "A Western Journey." It is really a kind of tremendous kaleidoscope that I hope may succeed in recording a whole hemisphere of life and of America.

This was part of the last letter I was ever to receive from Wolfe. Two days later he had pneumonia, from the complications of which he was to die in Johns Hopkins Hospital within nine weeks.

There in Baltimore, on that sad September fifteenth, a few hours after Wolfe had died, I sat in the hospital talking with the members of his family. The question of his unpublished manuscripts came up. I asked if they knew anything about "A Western Journey." His mother undertook to look through his bags. And there it was—a bound ledger of the kind used in simple bookkeeping; it was in just such ledgers as this that Wolfe had written his first longhand drafts of everything. The ledger was full to the last page of his almost illegible penciled scrawl, with the title, "A Western Journey," at the beginning. There were not fifty thousand words, nothing like it. Wolfe always used round numbers loosely. When he said, "I have written a million words," he meant: "I have written a lot." When he said, "I have written fifty thousand words," he meant: "I have written only a little; in fact, I have just started." It was the last manuscript which that large hand of the artist would ever write.

EDWARD C. ASWELL
Virginia Quarterly Review
Summer 1939

Foreword

The University of Pittsburgh Press, in January 1950, entered into a contract with Edward C. Aswell (Administrator, C.T.A., for the estate of Thomas Wolfe) to publish Wolfe's *Western Journal.*

This last writing of Thomas Wolfe's had been brought to the attention of the Press by Lawrence Lee, associate professor of English at the University of Pittsburgh, who had published a fragment of the *Journal* in the summer issue, 1939, of the *Virginia Quarterly Review* when he was editor of the *Review.*

From the Houghton Library, Harvard University, the Press got photostats of the *Journal* as it was written in the almost undecipherable handwriting of the author.

The *Journal* was kept daily from June 20 through July 2, 1938, while Wolfe was on a motor trip through national parks of eight western states. It was written with a soft pencil, late at night, after the long trip of the day was over, on the pages of a record book (National 1759½). In the book are 300 lined pages, 5½ x 8⅝, with one-inch margins marked off in red. *Record* is impressed in the middle of the front cover, and the book shows much wear.

For a few pages in the beginning of the book (1-9) Wolfe wrote on both left- and right-hand pages. From 9 through 215 he wrote on right-hand pages (except for 150, which is a page of figures); from 215 on through to 300 he wrote on all pages, both left- and right-hand. The sequence of the account of his journey, day after day, however, is not always to be read in the order of numbered pages. The account in sequence is to be read on both left- and right-hand pages through to 299, and then back on the left-hand pages (the even numbered pages) from 300 to 238. In spite of the *Journal's* turning back on itself as Wolfe wrote it, the calendar sequence from Monday June 20 through Saturday July 2 helps make clear the order and sequence of his writing.

Another confusion results from the writing on pages 4, 6, and the bottom of page 8. These fragments dated June 31, Spokane, are written among the records of June 20 and 21, on pages and in territory Wolfe had left behind many days before he reached Spokane. It seems probable they were written after the trip was over and after Wolfe had written on page 238 *End of the Trip*. In the first place, there is, of course, no June 31 in the calendar and there are accounts of June 30 and July 1 in the *Journal* where they belong. In the second place, the substance of these fragments dated June 31 is a kind of summary of impressions and reflections on the whole trip. For these reasons, the pages 4, 6, and the bottom part of 8 are printed at the end of the *Journal*. In any sense, actual or artistic, the final words on 8 are a more satisfying climax for the *Journal* than those on 238.

The *Journal* is almost never written in complete sentences. It is a series of phrases, even stray words, usually separated one from another by dashes. The "ands" which follow almost every dash or introduce any new impression seem not to be connectives but rather response to the "rolling of the white Ford" and to the tumbling eagerness of Wolfe's thoughts and feelings. It is as if always his mind ran faster than his pencil could.

The punctuation, the capitalization, and the paragraphing used in this book are Wolfe's. The spelling, because of the uncertainty about some letters and the shorthand method Wolfe often used, may be edited.

Where Wolfe himself used a question mark to show uncertainty about the names of towns, mountains, rivers, or the like, the map was consulted and the right name is given in notes at the end of the book, on page 75. The faithfulness with which Wolfe has recalled and recorded every turn in the road makes it not too difficult to trace on the map the very roads the white Ford traveled.

The *Journal* is printed here in full and, we believe, just as it was written. To decipher every word and try to be sure it was the word Wolfe wrote was the pleasant labor of many hours with my colleague Percival Hunt. His unflagging zeal and inspired "sleuthing" is responsible for discovering many words that might have remained forever a mystery. For both of us, I think, the very difficulties have made the author's tremendous intensity, his eagerness, intolerance, gentleness, and elemental poetry a very real "Itselfness" (as Wolfe might say)—an "Itselfness" which is there to enjoy, apart from any literary form, or lack of it, and apart from any agreement with the author's opinions.

At least, now that all the work is done—after the deciphering, the transcribing, the arranging, the mapping of the journey—the feeling persists that we have been very close to the power and genius of this writer and his writing. It has been like being right there when the spark flashes.

The original manuscript of this journal is from the William A. Wisdom Collection of the Houghton Library, and was used by permission of the Harvard College Library.

The map of Thomas Wolfe's journey was drawn by Dr. Frances M. Hanson, assistant professor of geography, and the decorative cartouche was drawn by Jeanette C. Shirk, periodicals librarian, University of Pittsburgh. The lettering was by Theodore Bowman.

Permission to quote from *The Story of a Novel* on page x was given by Charles Scribner's Sons.

AGNES LYNCH STARRETT
Editor, University of Pittsburgh Press
1951

Out of the billion forms of America, out of the savage violence and the dense complexity of all its swarming life; from the unique and single substance of this land and life of ours, must we draw the power and energy of our own life, the articulation of our speech, the substance of our art.

For here it seems to me in hard and honest ways like these we may find the tongue, the language, and the conscience that as men and artists we have got to have. Here, too, perhaps, must we who have no more than what we have, who know no more than what we know, who are no more than what we are, find our America. Here, at this present hour and moment of my life, I seek for mine.

THOMAS WOLFE
The Story of a Novel

. . . the pity, terror, strangeness, and magnificence of it all.

THOMAS WOLFE
A Western Journal

A Western Journal

By

Thomas Wolfe

Storm-herds of thundering Sioux cloud past in viewless vacancy. Long, long ago, within the anodes of the timeless West—a man felt, saw, heard, thought—or did he vision them—these things—Oh, time.

A Daily Log
of
the Great Parks Trip

Monday June 20. (Chester [illegible]) Left Portland, University Club 8:15 sharp — Fine day, bright sunlight no clouds in sky — went South by East through fields of upper Willamette and over some most food which was glorious in brilliant sun — Then climbed and crossed Cascades, and came down with

86 miles [illegible] of [illegible] onto the dry lands of the Eastern slope — then over high plateau and through bare hills and canyons and irrigated farming here and there, [illegible] etc. and into Bend at 12:45! — 200 miles in 4 1/2 hours —

Then lunch at hotel and view of the 3 Sisters and the Cascade range — then up to the Pilot Butte along the tower — the great plain shelf infinite away — and unparalleled the great line of the Cascades with their snow-capped summits Hood, Adams, Jefferson, 3 Sisters etc., and at [illegible] left Bend at 3 and then through the vast and level sunlands — [illegible] to the ~~South~~ for 100 miles & then down through the wild pine

A Daily Log of The Great Parks Trip

Monday June 20 (Crater Lake)

Left Portland, University Club, 8:15 sharp—Fair day, bright sunlight, no cloud in sky—Went South by East through farmlands of upper Willamette and around base of Mount Hood which was glowing in brilliant sun—Then climbed and crossed Cascades, and came down with suddenness of knife into the dry lands of the Eastern slope—Then over high plateau and through bare hills and canyons and irrigated farmlands here and there, low valley, etc., and into Bent at 12:45—200 miles in 4½ hours—

86 miles

Then lunch at hotel and view of the 3 Sisters and the Cascade range—then up to the Pilot Butte above the town—the great plain stretching infinite away—and unapproachable the great line of the Cascades with their snowspired sentinels Hood, Adams, Jefferson, 3 sisters, etc, and out of Bend at 3 and then through the vast and level pinelands—somewhat reminiscent of the South for 100 miles then down through the noble pines

5

to the vast plainlike valley of the Klamath?—the virgin land of Canaan all again—the far-off ranges—infinite—Oregon and the Promised Land—then through the valley floor—past Indian reservation—Capt Jack—the Modocs—the great trees open approaching vicinity of the Park—the entrance and the reservation—the forester—the houses—the great snow patches underneath the trees—then the great climb upwards— the foresting, administration—up and up again—through the passes the great plain behind and at length the incredible crater of the lake—the hotel and a certain cheerlessness in spite of cordialness —dry tongues vain-licking for a feast—the return, the cottages, the college boys and girls who serve and wait—the cafeteria and the souvenirs—the great crater fading coldly in incredible cold light—at

7

length departure—and the forest rangers down below—long, long talks—too long with them about "our wonders", etc—then by darkness the sixty or seventy miles down the great dim expanse of Klamath Lake, the decision to stay here for the night—3 beers, a shower, and this, reveille at 5:30 in the morning—and so to bed!

First day: 404 miles

8

The gigantic unconscious humor of the situation —C "making every national park" without seeing any of them—the main thing is to "make them"—and so on and on tomorrow

7

Tuesday June 21, 1938 (Yosemite)

Dies Irae: Wakened at 5:30—dragged weary bones erect, dressed, closed baggage, was ready shortly before six, and we were off again "on the dot"—at six oclock. So out of Klamath, the lakes red, and a thread of silver river in the desert, and immediately

9

the desert, sage brush, and bare, naked, hills, giant-molded, craterous, cupreous, glaciated blasted—a demonic heath with reaches of great pine, and volcanic glaciation, cupreous, fiendish, desert, blasted—the ruins of old settlers home-steads, ghost towns and the bleak little facades of long forgotten postoffices lit bawdily by blazing rising sun and the winding mainstreet, the deserted station of the incessant railway—all dominated now by the glittering snow—pale masses of

11

Mount Shasta—pine lands, canyons, sweeps and rises, the naked crateric hills and the volcanic

lava masses and then Mount Shasta omnipresent
—Mount Shasta all the time—always Mt. Shasta
—and at last the town named Weed (with a
divine felicity)—and breakfast at Weed at 7:45—
and the morning bus from Portland and the
tired people tumbling out and in for breakfast

13

and away from Weed and towering Shasta at
8:15—and up and climbing and at length into
the passes of the lovely timbered Siskiyous
and now down into canyon of the Sacramento
in among the lovely timbered Siskiyous and all
through the morning down and down and down
the canyon, and the road snaking, snaking
always with a thousand little punctual gashes,
and the freight trains and the engines turned
backward with the cabs in front

15

down below along the lovely Sacramento snaking
snaking snaking—and at last into the town of
Redding and the timber fading, hills fading,
cupreous lavic masses fading—and almost at
once the mighty valley of the Sacramento—as
broad as a continent—and all through the morn-
ing through the great floor of that great plain

like valley—the vast fields thick with straw
grass lighter

17

than Swedes hair—and infinitely far and
unapproachable the towns down the mountain
on both sides—and great herds of fat brown
steers in straw light fields—a dry land, with with
a strange hot heady fragrance and fertility—
and at last no mountains at all but the great
sun-bright, heat-hazed, straw-light plain and
the straight marvel of the road on which the
car rushes

19

on like magic and no sense of speed at 60 miles
an hour—At 11:30 a brief halt at———to look at
the hotel—and great palms now, and spanish
tiles and arches and pilasters and a patio in
the hotel and swimming pool—and on again and
on again across the great, hot, straw light plain,
and great fields mown new and scattered with
infinite bundles of baled hay and

21

occasional clumps of greenery and pastures and
house and barns where water is and as Sacramento
nears a somewhat greener land, more unguent,

and better houses now, and great fat herds of
steers innumerable and lighter and more sun—
ovenhot towns and at length through the heat-
haze the slopes of Sacramento and over an
enormous viaduct across a flat

23

and marshy land and planes flying, and then
the far flung filling stations, hot dog stores,
3 Little Pigs, and Bar B-Q's of a California
town and then across the Sacramento into town—
the turn immediate and houses new and mighty
palms and trees and people walking. and the
State house with its gold leaf dome
and spaghetti at the first Greeks that we find,
and on out again immediate—

25

pressing on—past state house—and past street
by street of leafy trees and palms and pleasant
houses and out from town now—but traffic
flashing past now—and loaded trucks and
whizzing cars—no more the lovely 50 mile
stretches and 60 miles an hour—but down across
the backbone of the state—and the whole backbone
of the state—cars and towns and farms
and people

27

flashing by—and still that same vast
billowy plain—no light brown now—the
San Joaquin Valley now—and bursting with
Gods plenty—orchards—peaches—apricots—
and vineyards—orange groves—Gods plenty of
the best—and glaring little towns sown thick
with fruit packing houses—ovenhot, glittering
in the hot and shining air—town

29

after town—each in the middle of Gods plenty—
and at length the turn at———toward Yosemite—
90 miles away—and a few miles from town the
hills again—the barren, crateric, lavic, volcanic
blasted hills—but signs now telling us we can't
get in now across the washed out road save
behind the conductor—and now too late—already
5 of six and the last conductor leaves

31

at six and we still 50 miles away—and telephone
calls now to rangers, superintendents and so
forth, a filling station and hot cabins, and the
end of a day of blazing heat and the wind
stirring in the sycamores about the cabins, and
on again now, and almost immediately the broken

ground, the straw light mouldings, the rises to
the crater hills and soon

33

among them—climbing, climbing into timber—
and down down down into pleasant timbered
mountain folds—get no sensation yet and winding
in and out—and little hill towns here and there
and climbing, climbing, climbing, mountain
lodges, cabins, houses, and so on, and now in
terrific mountain folds, close packed, precipitous,
lapped together and down and over, down again

35

along breath taking curves and steepnesses and
sheer drops down below into a canyon cut a
mile below by great knifes blade—and at the
bottom the closed gate—the little store—calls upon
the phone again, and darkness and the sending
notes, and at last success—upon our own heads
be the risk but we may enter—and we do—
and so slowly up

37

we go along the washed out road—finding it
not near so dangerous as we feared—and at
length past the bad end and the closed gate and
release—and up now climbing and the sound of
mighty waters in the gorge and the sheer black-

nesses of beetling masses and the stars—and
presently the entrance and the rangers house—
a free pass now—and up and up—and boles of
trees terrific, cloven rock above the road

39

and over us and dizzy masses night black as a
cloud, a sense of the imminent terrific and at
length the valley of the Yosemite; roads forking
darkly, but the perfect sign—and now a smell
of smokes and of gigantic tentings and enormous
trees and gigantic cliff walls night black all
around and above the sky-bowl of starred night—
and Currys Lodge and

41

smoky gaiety and wonder—hundreds of young
faces and voices—the offices, buildings stores,
the dance floor crowded with its weary hundreds
and the hundreds of tents and cabins and the
absurdity of the life and the immensity of all—
and 1200 little shop girls and stenogs and new-
weds and schoolteachers and boys—all, God
bless their

43

little lives, necking, dancing, kissing, feeling,
and embracing in the great darkness of the giant

redwood trees—all laughing and getting loved tonight—and the sound of the dark gigantic fall of water—so to bed!

And 535 miles today!

45

Wed June 22

Woke at 7:00 after sound sleep—water falling —girls voices, etc—Breakfast—and good one at cafeteria—after that visited waterfalls took photographs, talked to people, visited swell hotel —sent post cards, etc, and then on way out— by the South Wawona entrance—then beautiful rockrim drive down through wooded Sierras to foothills—the brilliant leafage of scrub pine— then the bay-bright gold of wooded big barks— then the bay-gold plain and bay-gold heat—a crowded lovely road—and Clovis—lunch there— then the ride up to the mountains again—the same approach as the day before—the bay-gold big barks—then cupreous masses—then forested peaks—then marvelous and precipitous ride upward and the great view back across the vast tangle of the Sierras—then Gen. Grant and the great trees—the pretty little girls—then the 30 mile drive along the ridge

47

to the Sequoia—and Gen. Sherman—and the giant trees—then straight thru to other entrance then down terrifically the terrific winding road—the tortured view of the eleven ranges—the vertebrae of the Sierras—then the lowlands—and straight highroad—no bends—and Visalia—then by dark straight down the valley—to Bakersfield—then East and desertwards across the Tehachapi range—the vertical brightness of enormous cement plants—and now at 1:30 in Mohave at desert edge—and tomorrow across the desert at 8:00 o'clock—and so to bed—and about 365 miles today.

46

At Bakersfield—enormous electric sign—Frosted Milk-shakes—A Drive-Inn—and girls in white sailor pantys serving drinks—I drank Frosted Lime, Miller a Coco-Cola float, etc.

49

Thursday June 23

Up at 7 o'clock in hotel at Mohave—and already the room hot and stuffy and the wind that had promised a desert storm the night before was still and the sun already hot and mucoid on the incredibly dirty and besplattered window panes—and a moments look of hot tarred roof and a dirty ventilator in the restaurant below and no moving life but the freight cars of S.P. rr—

*and a slow freight climbing past and weariness—
so up and shaved and dressed and gripped the
zipper and downstairs and the white-cream Ford
waiting and the two others—in the car—and to
the cafe for breakfast—eggs and pancakes,
sausages most hearty—and a company of r.r.
men—So out of town at 8:10 and headed straight
into the desert—and so straight across*

51

*the Mohave at high speed for four hours—to
Barstow—so in full flight now—the desert yet
more desert—blazing heat—102 inside the filling
station—the dejected old man and his wife—
and so the desert mountains, crateric, lavic and
volcanic, and so more fiendish the fiend desert
of the lavoid earth like an immense plain of
Librea tar—and very occasionally a tiny
blistered little house—and once or twice the
paradise of water and the magic greenery of
desert trees—and*

53

*yet hotter and more fiendish—through fried hills
—cupreous, ferrous, and denuded as slag heaps
—and so the filling station and the furnace air
fanned by a hot dry strangely invigorating breeze*

and the filling station man who couldn't sign
"I'm only up an hour and my hands shake so
with the heat"—and Needles at last in blazing
heat and the restaurant station and hotel and
Fred Harvey all aircooled, and a good luncheon,
and an hour here—

55

so out again in blazing heat—106° within the
strolling of the station awning—116 or 120 out
of it—and so out of Needles—and through heat
blasted air along the Colorado 15 miles or so
and then across the river into Arizona—pause
for inspection, all friendly and immediate—
then into the desert world of Arizona—the
heat blasted air—the desert mountain slopes clear
in view and more devilish—

57

the crateric and volcanic slopes down in and up
and up among them, now and then a blistered
little town—a few blazing houses and the fronts
of stores—up and up now and fried desert
slopes prodigiously—and into Oatman and the
gold mining pits, the craterholes, the mine shafts
and the signs of new gold digging—Mexicans
half naked before a pit—and up and up and
only up and up to Goldcrest?

58

Across the Mohave the S.P. fringed with black
against the blazing crater of the desert sky snakes
on, snakes on its monotone of forever and of
now—moveless Immediate

59

and at last the rim and down and down through
blasted slopes, volcanic "pipes" and ancient
sea erosions, mesa table heads, columnar swathes,
stratifications, and the fiendish wind, and below
the vast pale, lemon-mystic plain—and far
away immeasurably far the almost moveless
plume of black of engine smoke and the double
header freight advancing—advanceless moveless—
moving through timeless time and on and on
across the

61

immense plain backed by more immensities of
fiendish mountain slopes to meet it and so almost
meeting moveless-moving never meeting up and
up and round and through a pass and down to
Kingman and a halt for water and on and on
and up and down into another mighty plain,
desert growing grey-green greener—and some
cattle now and always up and up and through
fried blasted slopes and the enormous

63

lemon-magic of the desert plains, fiend mountain
slopes pure lemon heat mist as from magic
seas arising—and a halt for gas at a filling
station with a water fountain "Please be careful
with the water we have to haul it 60 miles"—
5280 feet above—and 4800 feet we've climbed
since Needles and on and on and up and the
country greening now and

65

steers in fields wrenching grey-green grass among
the sage brush clumps and trees beginning now—
the National Forest beginning—and new
greenery—and trees and pines and grass again
—a world of desert greenness still not Oregon—
but a different world entirely from the desert
world and hill slopes no longer fiend troubled
but now friendly, forested familiar, and around
and

67

down and in a pleasant valley Williams—and
for a beer here where I thought I was 3 years
ago—bartender a Mexican or an Indian or
both and out and on our way again only the
great road leading across the continent and 6 or
7 miles out an off turn to the left for the Grand

Canyon—and not much climbing now, but up
and down again the great plateau 7000 feet

69

on top—and green fields now and grass and steers
and hills forested and cooler and trees and on
and on toward (levelly) the distant twin rims—
blue-vague defined—of the terrific canyon—
the great sun sinking now below our 7000 feet—
we racing on to catch him at the canyon ere he
sinks entirely—but too late, too late—at last
the rangers little house, the

71

permit and the sticker, the inevitable conversations,
the polite goodbyes—and (almost dark now)
at 8:35 to the edges of the canyon—to Bright
Angel Lodge— and before we enter between the
cabins of the Big Gorgooby—and the Big
Gorgooby there immensely, darkly, almost
weirdly there—a fathomless darkness peered at
from the very edge of hell with abysmal starlight—
almost unseen—just

73

fathomlessly there—So to our cabin—and
delightful service—and so to dinner in the Lodge

—and our rudeeleven in jodphurs, pajamas, shirts, and country suits, and Fred Harvey's ornate wigwam—and to dinner here—and then to walk along the rim of Big Gorgooby and inspect the big hotel—and at the stars innumerable and immense above the Big Gorgooby just a look—a big look—so goodnight and 500 miles today—

75

Friday
June 24, 1938

At daybreak a deer outside the window cropping grass.

Rose Grand Canyon 8:15—others had been up already for an hour—wakened at four or thereabouts by deer grazing, and by its hard small feet outside of window—Then Miller in at 8:30—but let me sleep—so bathed, dressed, to coffee shop by G and good breakfast then packed and with Miller Conway and the Ranger to Administration offices, met the Ass't Super.—so to Observation point—the Ranger along and looked through observation glasses at

77

Old Gorgooby and unvital time—and Alberdene the young geologist with crisp-curly hair and cheery personality who talked and remembered me from 3 yr. ago—an Arizona PhD and at

Harvard too—but now wants no more teaching and applies for Philippines—so down to Lookout Tower where the caravan streams in and listens to lecture by young Ranger Columbia and into tower and all the people—the Eastern cowboy with Fred Harvey hat and

79

shirt and cowgirl with broad hat, and wet red mouth, blonde locks and riding breeches filled with buttock—and up into tower and the Painted Desert and the Small Gorgooby gorge—and the Vermillion Cliffs—and down and goodbye to the ranger—and so away—and stop over for a look at Small Gorgooby gorge—and on to the desert and to Cameron and blazing

81

heat and the demented reds again, and lunch here in an Indian Lodge-ee —and an old dog moving in the shadow of a wall—and so away across the bridge and into the Painted Desert and blazing heat and baked road and Painted Desert through the afternoon by the Vermillion Cliffs—and four small Indian girls in rags and petticoats beside the road awaiting

83

pennies (dimes they got) two upon a burro—
beer, and photographs and heat incredible and the
demented reds of Painted Desert and away away
again good road—bad road—good and bad again
by the demented and fiend tortured redness of
Vermillion Cliffs—red, mauve, and violet,
passing into red again—and now the gorge,
much smaller down, of Big

85

Gorgooby, and the Navajo Bridge—and the
Gorgooby, brown-red-yellow—a mere 1000 feet or
so below—and on and on across the Big Gorgooby
now through desert land—now grey-greening
sagely into sage and stray Indians moving into
road here and there and Indian houses—then
the far lift of the rise, the road rising, winding
into hills, and up and up into

87

the timber and the forest now, and all the lovely
quaking aspens and the vast and rising rim of
sage and meadow land—a golf course big and
narrow on both sides—rising clearly and
mysteriously to woods—and then the big woods
again, and deep dense woods, the rangers house
and entrance, and at last the Lodge, the
mysterious colour, a haircut, a clean

89

shirt, and supper with the Browns, and a sweet
waitress, and before this past—the sunset
moment—the tremendous twilight of the Big
Gorgooby—more concise and more collected,
more tremendous here—and dimmer then and
darkness and the lights of the South Rim—
and later on the moving picture the two Canadian
College quartettes in crimson blazers—the
inevitable theatrical performance with the

91

waitresses and bellhops performing—Hiawatha
chanting the U.P.—and naught but the clog
dancers passable—and then Brown and his
colored picture slides—Bryce, Zion, the Canyon,
and the Mormon temple, then the dance, the bar,
Scotch highballs, and good talk with Miller, and
the wind in pine trees, and leave with Miller
to the cabin, and

93

C. still wakeful, rising, reading costs and
mileages excitably from his records—he all the
night with them—and arguments, agreements,
and accounts again on costs and mileages and
possibilities—the moon in 30 hrs. is possible—
and C taking pride in all our present luxury

because "It makes a better person of you" and the first time he gave a

95

man a tip—and so to bed! And 210 miles today

97

Saturday June 25, 1938

Rose 7:30 cabin North Rim Lodge Grand Canyon—shave, bath, dressed—Cabin very luxurious—appointed like modern hotel—best we'd seen—Sound of waitresses and maids singing farewell songs—"Till we meet again" etc—to passengers departing on buses—Traveling U.P. sentiment and C declared there were tears in eyes of the passengers and some of the girls—Into Lodge for view from terrace of the Big Gorgooby in first light—and glorious—! and glorious!—wrote half dozen post cards in brilliant sunlight as before—then into breakfast with C and M and

99

the Browns—and the inevitable Ranger—and the waitress with the strange and charming smile—and she from Texas and admitted that sentiment, songs, and kicking her legs for Pony Boy in night time entertainment all at 8000 feet for

dear old U.P. got her wind and at first "made
her awfully tired"—So out and by myself again
to terrace—then to cabin to pack—then to hotel—
and with Ranger and C and M to cafeteria for
the inevitable inspection of cabins, cafeterias,
etc—and at long last, at 11 o'clock

101

on our way out—and down through the Forest,
and the long sweeping upland meadows and the
deer and cattle grazing, quivering the aspen leaves
in the bright air, and down and down and then
the bottomlands spread below us over again, the
fierce red earth, the tortured buttes and the
Vermillion Cliffs, the Painted desert, and on and
on across the desert and into Utah, and at 1:30,
3 miles past the

103

line, the Mormon town of Kanab at Perry's
Lodge—a white house, pleasant and almost
New England, and the fiery bright heat, the little
town, and greenness here, and trees and grass,
and a gigantic lovely cool-bright poplar at the
corner—and so out and on along the road and
presently the turn off to the left for Zion's
Canyon—and before the mountains rising range
and range, no longer

105

fierce red and vermillion now, but sandy, whitest
limestones, striped with strange stripes of salmon
pink—scrub dotted, paler—Now in the canyon
road and climbing, and now pink rock again,
strange shapes and scarings in the rock, and
even vertices upon huge swathes of stone, and
plunging down now in stiff canyon folds the
sheer solid beetling

107

soaplike block of salmon red again—deeper yet
not so fierce and strange (as I thought) as the
Grand Canyon earth, and towering soapstone
blocks of red incredible, and through a tunnel,
out and down and down, and through the great
one spaced with even windows in the rock that
give on magic casements opening on sheer blocks
of soapstone red, and out again

109

in the fierce light and down round dizzy windings
of the road into the canyons depth and at the
bottom halt inevitable at Administration Offices,
visit inevitable to cafeteria and cabins, and away
again along the canyon and the Virgin River
(how sweet to see sweet water sweetly flowing here
between these dizzy soapstone blocks of red)
and round

111

the bendings of the river by the soapstone walls of
blank fierce red and into the valley floor and trees
(a little like Yosemite, this valley, yet not so
lush, so cool, nor so enchanted, nor cooled by the
dunblanket of towering pines, but an oasis here,
a glimpse of lodge inevitable and—O miracle!—
in hot oasis a swimming pool, a bathing house,
and young wet half-naked forms—a pool
surrounded

113

by the cottonwoods and walled round, beetled over
by sheer soapstone blocks of red capped by
pinnicles of blazing white—O pool in cottonwoods
surrounded by fierce blocks of red and temples
and kings thrones and the sheer smoothness of the
bloody vertices of soapstone red—did never pool
look cooler, nor water wetter, wetter more inviting
—so by

115

the road down to the canyons end and all around
the beetling blocks of soapstone red, and river
flowing, and trees and shade, a tourist party,
and a lecturer—and two old friends—and one
from Saginaw and one from somewhere else,
and one a coal salesman, and one something else,

and one with an enormous belly and a half-sleeved shirt, the other with

117

green-visored helmet, and two fingers only on his hand, and both amiable and voluble and willing to pose, and talk and act, and awed by nature dutifully—and so amiably goodbye to them, back to the swimming pool, and snapshots here, and so away, and a shot at a white lime-cliff on the way, and up and up again, and through the tunnel, and by the

119

strange carved shapes and vertical and punctual lines, and to the top and down and down again a vista of the plain and desert, and the white sand-lime peaks with the salmon markings—and one strange, isolate and Painted Desertward (I think) of salmon red and down and down and to the main road finally and to the left and up along it toward Bryce's Canyon on the main

121

road north to Salt Lake City—and now, almost immediate, a greener land, and grass in semi-desert fields, and stock and cattle grazing, and now timbered hills in contour not unlike the fields of home, and now farms and green incredible of fields and hay and mowing and things growing and green trees and Canaan pleasantness and a river flowing (the

123

Sevier) and (by desert comparison) a fruitful valley—and occasional little towns—small Mormon towns—sometimes with little house of old brick—but mostly little houses of frame, and for the most part mean and plain and stunted looking and hills rising to the left—a vista of salmon pink, Vermillion Cliffs again—the barricades of Bryce—and

125

then the turn in—and so halted here by road repair until the convoy from the Canyon passes out—and meanwhile talking to the man with the red flag—"we have no deserts here in Utah"—is Zion then a flowering prairie, and are Salt Lake and the Bonneville Flats the grassy precincts of the King's Paradise—and cars gathered here on bleeding oil—

127

from Ohio—New Mexico—Illinois—California—Michigan—and presently the other cavalcade appears upon the crest and flash downwards one by one till all are through—and then we start—the road good but still oil-bloody to the right for seven or ten miles—and up through sage land into timber, past corrals, dude ranches etc, into

129

timber on the high plateau, another Rangers entrance house in view, the stick-candy-whipping of the flag—another sticker—seven now—and into the park and up and through the timber past the Lodge and to the river, where stand in setting sun looking out and down upon the least overwhelming, dizzy, and least massive of the lot—but perhaps

131

the most astounding—a million wind-blown pinnacles of salmon pink and fiery white all fused together like stick candy—all suggestive of a childs fantasy of heaven and beyond the open semi-green and semi-desert plain—and lime-white and scrub dotted mountains—and so back and to the Lodge with sour-pussed oldsters on the veranda, trinkets

133

souvenirs, and, methought, some superciliousness within, so got our keys, and to our cabin, and so shaved, and to the cafeteria which was clean and much be-Indian-souvenired betrinketed, somehow depressing, and expensive—pie ten 15 cents and 20 for a bad and messy sandwich—and so to the Lodge and peeked in at the inevitable Ranger and the attentive

135

dutiful sourpusses listening to the inevitable lecture—Flora and Fauna of Bryce Canyon—so bought post cards and wrote them—and so to my cabin to write this.

And after this to lodge where dinner going on, and into curio shop where, with some difficulty bought beer in cans, and had two, feeling more and more desolate in this most unreal state of Utah, and

137

struck up talk with quaint old blondined wag named Florence who imitates bird calls and dark rather attractive woman, Canadian probably French, who sold curios and who had life in her —and was obviously willing to share it—So talking with them in lobby until dinner broke up at 10:30 and young people coming out looking rather lost and vaguely eager, I thought, as if they wanted something that wasn't there and didn't know how

139

to find it—and had some depressing reflections on Americans in search of gaiety, and National Park Lodges, and Utah and frustration, etc; so home, where found C busy with his calculations —"if we do so and so tomorrow, we'll have only so and so much to do on Monday"—and wrote this, my companions sleeping—and so to bed!

About 265 miles today!

141

Sunday
June 26, 1938

Arose Bryce Canyon 7:30 dressed, walked with M to Rim and to observation house on point and looked at Canyon. Sky somewhat overcast and no sunlight in the canyon, but it was no less amazing —looked fragile compared to other great canyons "like filigree work", of fantastic loveliness Great shouldering bulwarks of eroded sand going down to it—made it look very brittle and soft—erodes at rate of 1 inch a year—something the effect of sugar candy at a carnival—powdery—whitey—melting away—Old man, roughly dressed, and with one tooth, and wife, and daughter, suprisingly smart looking young female in pajama slacks and smoked goggles talking geology—

143

the words came trippingly off her tongue—"erosion"—"wind erosion"—"125 million years *and so on"—There had been argument with someone whether Canyon had been cut with water —"all canyons cut with water" etc—M took pictures "Look out as if you're looking out"— then quickly back through woods toward lodge and after last nights rain brightly amazingly pungent, sweet and fragrant—smell of sage, pine needles, etc—So breakfast in lodge and C as usual engrossed with hotel manager haggling about prices, rates, cabin accommodations etc—wrote*

145

post cards and ate hearty breakfast and talked with waitress who was from Purdue—studying "home economics" and dress designing and hopes to be a "buyer" for Chicago store—observed the tourists—two grim featured females—school-teachers—at table next—who glowered dourly at everyone and everything with stiff inflexible faces and H. says most of the tourists are women and many school teachers—So the tourists rose to depart, and presently the sound of singing and the waitresses, maids, bell boys etc gathered in front of Lodge and by bus singing

147

"Till we meet again"—"Good-bye, ladies" etc— and one of the dour looking school teachers

dabbing furtively at eyes, and the bus departing, and emotional farewells, and the young folks departing back to their work, and bragging exultantly "We got tears out of four of 'em this morning. Oh, I love to see 'em cry; it means business"—Then discussing hotel business again and the art of pleasing guests and squeezing tears from them—and for me the memory of

149

the dour faced teacher dabbing at her eyes and stabbing pity in the heart and something that can not be said—So into hotel for a final look, and boys and girls practising the dances of a show, so to the cabin packed, back to the lodge and farewell conversation with the curio-saleslady of last night, and with the managers wife—and so farewell—and checked out the gates at 9:45 and down from the canyon

151

through the woods, past the lodge-motor-cabin Start outside, on to the road-in-construction slowly, down towards the valley, and finally (15 miles away) into the main road for Salt Lake and toward North—and Salt Lake from this point 250 miles away.—

So all through the morning at good speed upon fine roads up through a great, enlarging, and constantly growing richer valley—at first mixed with some

153

desert land—bald, scrub dotted ridges on each side ascending into lovely timber then to granite tops, and desert land now semi-desert, semi-green—clumped now with sage and dry, but bursting marvellously into greenery when water is let in—and the river (the Sevier) refreshing it. Still semi desert with occasional flings into riper green—the cool dense green of trees

155

clustered densely round a little house, and fields ripe with thick green, and the warm green of hay, and fat steers and cows and horses grazing, apparent men are Mormon   Sickling reaping, mowing hay with reaping machines and fields strewn with cut mounds of green lemon hay, and water—the miraculousness of water in the west, the muddy viscousness of irrigation

157

ditches filled with water so incredibly wet—the miracle of water always in the west—the blazing

whiteness of the sunlight now, the light hot
blueness of the skies, the piled cumulousness of
snowy clouds—and then the dusty little Mormon
villages—blazing and blistered in that hot dry
heat—and the forlorn little houses—sometimes
just little

159

cramped and warped wooden boxes, all unpainted,
hidden under the merciful screenings of the dense
and sudden trees—the blistered little storefronts,
the wooden falsefronts of the little towns—
sometimes the older Mormon houses of red brick—
sometimes still more ancient ones of chinked log
—sometimes strangely an old Mormon house of
stone—but all in that hot dry immensity

161

of heat and light so curiously warped and small
and dusty and forlorn—just a touch of strange-
ness maybe in the set of eaves, the placing of the
tag porch, the turn of the shop gables (temple-wise
perhaps)—but of architecture graceless, all
denuded, with the curious sterility and coldness
and frustration the religion has—but the earth
meanwhile

163

burgeoning into green and fat fertility—the windbreaks of the virgin poplars, the dense cool green of poplars in the hot bright light and the staunch cool shade of cottonwoods—and the valley winding into Canaan and the Promised land—the fields lush now with their green, their planted trees, the great reap of their mowings—strangely Canaan

165

now—hemmed by the desert peaks—the hackled ridges on both sides—denuded and half barren, curiously thrilling in their nakedness—and Canaan magical, the vale irriguous below—The marvellous freshness and fecundity of the great Sevier valley now and in the midst of the great plain of Canaan the town of Richfield (so named because of the

167

fat district)—a stop here—so on steadily into growing fertilities—a blessed land of Canaan irriguous—by L.D.S. made fertile, promised, and 'This is the place'—Jacob, Levan, Nephi, Goshen—the names Biblical in Canaan—or Spanish Fork and American Fork—names like the pioneers—but ever the towns arising from the desert

169

now—the lightness of new brick—the stamped
hard patterns of new bungalows—and in the
bright hot light clear wide streets, neat houses, an
air of growing and of prosperousness—but still
a graceless lack of architectural taste—but now a
kind of cooler sterner magic in the scenery
(impassionate, granite, clearly barren in the

171

hackled ridges of the limestone peaks, the austere
blackness of the timber)—and the great valley
floor burgeoning with Canaan in between—the
cool flat silver of the lake at Provo and the full
fat land of plenty now—cherry orchards groaning
with their fruit, fields thick with grain and hay,
and

173

fertile tillages betwixt the granite semi-arid
clearness of the desert peaks—Provo—its
thriving look—the immense smelter plants—in
hot bright air the hot bright sunlight of the
business street, the ugly sparseness, stamped out
smartness of the stamped brick bungalows— the
marvellousness of poplars and of cottonwoods,
the

175

dazzling brightness, richness, fragrance of the rambler roses—and full fat land of Canaan all away—great canning plants now, and fine wide roads, and flashing and increasing traffic—and Brighams great vale irriguous of Canaan and of plenty is marching, marching Northward between hackled peaks, is sweeping, sweeping Northward

177

through the backbone of the Promised Land, is sweeping onward, onward toward the Temple and the Lake—and by a rise approaching the barriers of the hackled peak, up, up, around the naked shoulder of a gravel mountain and down, down into the salt plain of Salt Lake—half-desert still, half burgeoning to riches and

179

the irriguous ripe of the sudden green, and walled immensely on three sides by the hackled grandeur of the massive hills—but to the West, the massive peaks also but desert openness and the saline flatness, the thin mist lemon of the Great Salt Lake—so now the houses thicken on both sides—another town with hot bright

181

central street, and stores, and city hall and, like the others, a denuded absence of humanity—

then down four miles away to Salt Lake City—the bungalows close-set now on both sides—suddenly—heat—heat-misty on its splendid rise and facing the approach backed by the naked molding of the hills—the Capitol—with its

183

dome—looking like a capital and dome always do—So into Salt Lake—skyscrapers, hotels, office buildings, an appearance of a City greater than its growth and in 4 directions the broad streets sweeping out and ending cleanly under massed dense green at the rises of the barren magic hills—so into town, past a fantastic dance hall, "the worlds

185

biggest"—stores, streets, blocks 600 feet in length and Sunday hotness, brightness, emptiness—the old feeling of Mormon coldness, desolation—the cruel, the devoted, the fanatic, and the warped and dead.

So for a hearty dinner at Rotisserie, then to the gleaming whiteness of Utah Hotel, the ornate hotel lobby, and mail for C and M. Then out into the garden around

187

the Temple—the harsh ugly temple, the temple sacrosanct, by us unvisited, unvisitable, so ugly, grim, grotesque, and blah—so curiously warped, grotesque, somehow so cruelly formidable—then the great domed roof of the Tabernacle like a political convention hall—the statues of the twin saints Brothers Smith, with pious recordings of their fanaticisms—

189

the museum, the first cabin, etc—the pompositities of bronze rhetoric—the solemn avowals of "the finding of the plates" for the Book of Mormon, etc—a visit to The Lion House, The Bee Hive, and so forth—and enough, enough, of all this folly, this cruelty and this superstition—into the white car now and out of town—almost

191

immediate the clear and naked hill beside and to the left the vast meadows sloping to pale flatness, and the saline, citric flatness paleness of the lake —And Land of Plenty now indeed—to the right the hackled, semi barren ridges, and a strip of arid land, then marvellously the orchards, on both

193

sides the orchards lusty with their fruit, their vineyards growing with their cherries, and

greenery, lushness, watery fertility, the like of
which was never seen before, flanked in the
distance by the pale and misty flatness of the
lake, the land merging into saline flatness at
the margin and beyond the misty range of the
hackled peaks—aye,

195

with the cruelty of Mormon in it, but with a
quality its own that grips and holds you now—
and thriving towns Ogden—"the fastest growing
city in Utah"—and flashing brightness and an
air of prosperousness and the clear elevation of
the bald and hackled peaks—and ever greater
orchards groaning with their fruit, and canning
plants,

197

and lush fertility—and Brigham, another
thriving and exciting lively town—the strange
tabernacled form of the Mormon temple with
its 8 gables on each side—but before we enter the
lively main street just before us—a turn-off to
the left—and almost immediate a climb up to the
hills and over them

199

and down the canyons toward Logan—and now
the greatest beauty of the day—the swift mounting

up the canyon among bold and greening knobs,
a sense of grandeur, sweetness and familiarity,
and suddenly, cupped in the rim of bold hills, a
magic valley plain, flat as a floor and green as
heaven and more

201

fertile and more ripe than the Promised land
then down and winding down the lovely canyon
and cattle, horses, and houses sheltered by the
trees, and then below the most lovely and
enchanted valley of them all—the great valley
around Logan—a valley that makes all that has
gone before fade to nothing—the

203

very core and fruit of Canaan—a vast sweet
plain of unimaginable riches—loaded with fruit,
lusty with cherry orchards, green with its thick
and lush fertility and dotted everywhere with the
beauty of incredible trees—clumped cottonwoods
and lines and windbreaks of incredible poplars—

205

a land of peace and promises of plenty—and then
Logan, a thriving, light town, blazing with electric
light and an air of cheerfulness—the fresh

bungalows and cottages and the more expensive
houses—the tabernacle, and with a curious
tightening of the throat, a thought of little
Alladine who lived here, loved it and its canyon,

207

and went out like a million other kids like her,
from all this Canaan loveliness to her future,
fame and glory in the city—and so out and on,
light climbing now, and along that valley
incredible, and at length across the line to Idaho,
and into Preston, blazing with Idaho's electric
light—and here perhaps lost the true road, for

209

we entered now a very rough one "under con-
struction for twenty miles"—and hunted in the
darkness with a sense of strangeness and it had
rained here and to the North the sky was murky
rent with gigantic flashes of Western lightning—
and the road perilous and slippery, too, the car
sliding sideways as on hills of snow—but we
slogged

211

through it to the good road and so on, between
hogback ridges that had closed on us, through

what was now, I suspect, desert country, towards Pocatello—on a splendid road—where we arrived just before eleven—registered at the Bannock hotel—out in brightly lighted streets and colorful victuallers for food—a sandwich and some beer—so home

213

most tired—the others sleeping soundly now—perhaps somewhat too fatigued by the crowded beauty, splendor and magnificence of this day to write it down—and so to bed!

And today 467 miles! (and in our first seven days about 2760 of our journey)

215

Monday June [*27, 1938*]

Up at 8:10—Pocatello—overcast sky—dressed, shaved, etc—down for breakfast in coffee shop (Banock Hotel)—C and M already there—so out of Pocatello and two miles out found we had left maps, books, etc—

So back—so finally out about 9:45 and the Sauriac peaks about the town—the bold naked skyways

But all through the morning through the great fertile valley of the Snake

and tired — ~~the~~
others sleeping really
now — perhaps remember
~~two~~ ~~[illegible]~~ fatigued
by the ~~[illegible]~~ wonderful beauty
splendor and magnificence
of this day to ~~write~~
it elsewhere — and
so to bed!

and today 467
miles! (and in perfect
seven days about 2760
of our journey)

feel and smell of sky
and beyond the horizons

the two streets, exploited
towns
the little unsorted
houses
the farms lonely, scattered
together in the vast
immense landscape
the towns — plastered —
little blasted houses — gray
exploited stores — the
big  of grain elevators
etc —
and water water
everywhere — beside the
road in fields in
[illegible] ditches, under

216

Following the train—the Yellowstone Express up through the Snake Valley—city streets—the towns—the whistling at the crossing—the final stop at—?—

The potato storage sheds sod roofed on top

The barns with the open loft door and the orchard

The piles of dark straw hay—the stockades, the cattle and the farms, the

217

most fertile we had seen perhaps—the foliage dense—the field green thick and natural—beside the road the thick and vernal greenness, lushness, freshness—by the irrigation ditches the thick and vernal growth almost middle western

218

feel and smell of clay and hay and stockades

The low sheds unpainted taverns

The little blistered house

The farm buildings curiously forgotten in the vast curious landscape

The towns—blistered—little blistered houses—farm implement stores—the big   of grain elevators etc—

and water water everywhere—beside the road in fields, in irrigation ditches, under

220

bridges—wetness of water flowing to the tops full to the floor of bridges magical full water brown-mud-yellow—marvellous everywhere

At Sugar City the turn off for Jackson Hole—the rises now and then another valley less vast but irriguous upon the western borders of the Tetons

"Almost a hole itself" says C—and truly almost

222

"holed" but open to one side—and find the pass through—then up up up but first through pined and hemlocked hyperboliac—the pleasant foldings of the hills—and pouring waters and then the steep turnings and the winds the vision of the timber line and snow and then the Pass and down below the miracle of Jackson

224

Hole—the milky winding of Cottonwood Creek and the Hole (and wild west enchantments and the bad-men legendries) terrific—and so down to it—and into Jackson—the Square of Old West now beduded—the western hands by the filling station—smell of horsewet hay, a thought of manure, and giggling kids upon two broncs—

luncheon in a "coffee shop"—the waitress and a blond rouged wryneck woman—and so out and round the

226

turn again, and up the edges of the valley by the Tetons and Leigh Lake and ? Lake and Jackson Lake—the park entrance, the museum, the glacial lake; the vastness and the sweetness and the Tetons; then through the Teton Forest, and Moran, and up and through the Forest hemlock, pine and spruce

228

by winding single road, and out of Forest and immediate beginning Yellowstone, and the Park entrance, and the ride up through pine-hemlock etc trees and then the Snake River foaming in its canyon, then a lake with the thick forest round it then the "Thumb" of Yellowstone, the Paint Pots and

230

the boiling waters, sinister, grotesque, curved like a rhinocerous imbedded moving through hot oatmeal—then by narrow road to Old Faithful, and a bear by privy and the woods, and smoke boiling from the ground, and then the vast bouquet of Old Faithful, the enormous Inn, the

232

tremendous lodges, the cabins—our run by the small fast flowing river—and the Crater lid, volcanic, the earth smoking from a hundred holes, and old Geyser and the people waiting, the hot boiling overslopping of the pot, and then the vast hot plume

234

of steam and water—and the people watching—Middle-America watching—kids, old men, women, young men, women—all—and the hot plume, the tons of water falling and the hot plume dipping—so to supper at the Lodge—and drinks first—and all the supper one could eat $1.00—and from the window

236

the hot plume again—and then the expectation—entertainment in the vasty hall—and roaring fire in lobby—and old people reading—and so goodnight to Ray—and then to dance and people dancing—so to the Great Inn to the bar—like liner shipboard bar—more merriment here and people more prosperous less cultured and singing "We don't give a damn for the whole state of Utah"

238

—and so talking and drinking with M.—and present the bar closes—midnight—and the rain ceased—the night cleared to heaven and a billion stars and to our lodge and to our cabin—Ray awake and talking all together—so to bed.

239

Up at 8:40—chill and cold—and maids talking at cabin door—and M in to wake me—So dressed and to cafeteria—and C waiting outside cabin making notes in book (his closeness, unstinting watchfulness, irked me) to cafeteria with him then—he having eaten—then all to Old Faithful where people coming in as from 1892 and talking to a man from Kansas, then Old Faithful squirted. So on our way along ***Tuesday June 28***

241

the crater basins—the hot fiery bubblings of the tormented bowels of earth—the Sapphire Pool—etc—people people people ("Don't lean on that. I'll have a parboiled boy" said man)—to geyser swimming pool before—father teaching child to float, etc—on our way to middle Basin, and on to Norris basin and Museum (not staying long here)—so cars by Canyon

243

road, enchanted country, and green meadows, and pine—hemlock—spruce—aspen forests—bears upon the road and lovely streams and water water in the west—Virginia cascades cascading—and the meadows and the Elk feasting and the bears now prowling on the road—all cars stopping—drivers automobiles stepping out to photograph a bear—so picked

245

up parking couple for a photo. She worked at Canyon hotel—so to Canyon Cafeteria—where lunch—and so across the Bridge to see the mighty falls of Yellowstone and water falling boiling and the rushing current of the Canyons loveliest stream—so clear and bright and pure compared to Colorado—so photographs and Ranger posing (for himself perhaps) with opera glasses

247

the steep wooded depths, the somewhat yellow walls (hence Yellowstone)—So back across the Bridge (no stopping for Bear Feeding now—no time) and then to Inspiration Point and the walk out over wavering upon the dizzy wooden Bridge—so on toward Mammoth Hot Springs—and the great climb and enchanted mountain country

249

now and great peaks to the west, and the climb,
the patched dirty snow beneath the trees and then
the rising eminence of Mount Washburn (?)—
and the timber line, the snow, the dizzy steepness
to the left, and the descent, the Buffalos like dots
grazing to the right—the elk—the enchanted
valleys far

251

below—now hackled crag peaks to the north and
west, and down and down—and then the halt at
Teton Falls, and the clear smoking silver of the
fall into the river—and then on, and buffalo
again—and the Elk Creeks—and finally below
the whited—mined-out bleakness of the Mammoth
Springs—and naked

253

cabins huddled into rows, and the blistered
erosions of the springs, the Lodges, the old Bldgs
of the Army Post, the vast slag-barrenness of
Everts Mountain and a sense of bleakness—and
the ranger and the talk the greeting and the
answers and with the ranger up to see the
Mammoth Springs, the colored rocks, the

255

terraces—and all bleak and disappointing and
so down and goodbye the ranger and the Army

Post and elk bones piled in decorative heaps and
post cards written hastily and out and out and
farewell Yellowstone and Gardner—a photo of
the car at the stone arch erected in 1872 (twas
said) and Gardner small and somewhat bleak and

257

like the entrance of a Nat'l Park with a string of
pullman cars that came up in the morning and
two pullman porters coming down the street, a
few stores advertising camp and fish equipment
and away from Gardner now along the Valley of
the Yellowstone and at first the bleak denuded
hills the rushing river the clear fast fish-
abundant river—and

259

then widening, and the naked hills enlarging into
rocky crags and forested (the timber deeper now
than Utah—and the material granite now no
longer limestone) and the valley greener now with
the widening and clear watered rush of Yellow-
stone—and an enchanted valley now with upslope
to the East and

261

right and timbered Rockies going into snow and
granite and the crags, nude spaciousness, and the

valley not so green as Mormon land mayhap—
but thick with greenness yellowed somewhat by the
teeth of steers, and the nude ranges going toward
the timbered crags and to the

263

west the miracle of evening light and the celebrated
river called the Yellowstone and trees most green
and marvellous—a scene familiar and unknown
and elements like those before in Mormon land
but by some miracle transformed into this Itself-
ness—and barns now

265

painted red upon the upland rank of ranges to
the East and fading light—and so to Livingston
like places known and come to before and supper
at the N.P. station and the waitress with the tired
face, and yet with charm, sedateness, and intelli-
gence, and the strange wood of

267

old trees and the station and in the big room the
free pamphlets of the L.D.S. and Christian
Science and Adventists and outside the walls of
rain (the moaning of full rivers lapping at the
rear) and blaze of neons, bars, and the bold hills
about—so out and to the West, the Yellowstone
and ripe greenery behind now

269

and the bold ridges closing in, the rise across the Bozeman Pass, a pause to read of Bozeman, Lewis, Clarke, and then the steep descent, the N.P. descending steeply with us, and ascending too, the double header climbing to the right above the cut, and then the lights of Bozeman—the broad main street

271

ablaze with power of brightness and abundant light, the hotel and then out with M to Bar and talk with Barkeep of Montana (and no depression said he) and so home with M; and said goodnight; so out again, and to another bar, the power flashing off, most sinister, the town in darkness and

273

queer in the bar around me, then out to first bar again, and then to cafe for hamburger, milk, etc., and then home—and this, and this—and so to bed!

275

Wednesday
June 29
(Glacier Park)

Up at seven—and downstairs—and breakfast with others—then off at 7:20 through valley with Bridger Mt's. on right, Rockies on left—and so sweeps of range—"a long county"—and presently

the great range with great sweeps—the mountains
fading to the right behind, the giant Rockies to
the right—and forestry and the signs and stops
to read them—and Helena and the enormous gold

277

dredge in Last Chance swinging up the hill—
then through the pass and over and the valleys
and the Gates of the Rockies, etc.—and the bank-
full Missouri and so on and at Wolf Creek away
again and climbing and now the vast Range—
the mountains to the left—the Continental—and
past the desert mouldings of the earth to the
right-before—the

279

immense and lovely grey green of the range and
great herds grazing—the straight backs of the
steers in the bright light and steak grazing on the
rump—and the Great American Plain opening
with infinite lift and rise and vastness to the
fore—so towards the Rockies and the lift and rise
and heaving of the Earth Mass—so the Blackfoot
reservation turn and Browning—all confused

281

disorderly and Indian—so on and on directly
toward the shining and bright austerity of the

mountains now and through the big barks and into the canyons—timber, right away, and in the mountains—and presently the town of Glacier Lake—and a sandwich there at the hotel—away and up the Lake again to Babb for mail—and back again from St. Mary's crossing and the cabins along the

283

Going to the Sun Pass and the stupendous hackled peaks now—the sheer basaltic walls of glaciation, the steep scoopings down below, the dense vertices of glacial valley slopes and forest—and climbing climbing to the Logan Pass so down again terrifically, and the glacial wall beside, the enormous hackled granite peaks before, the green steep

285

glaciation of the forest, the pouring cascades, and the streams below—and down and down the miraculous road into the forest, and by rushing waters, and down and down to the McDonald Lake and Hotel—and a cabin here beside the lake—and Ed away upon the waiting Lake steamer and Ray and I to cabin—then to dinner —there meeting Mr. Jack

287

Keyes—Ray's friend—then all together for a space—a drink with Keyes—and beer for Keyes and Miller in the cafeteria—and then all departing, all going, very tired and very sleepy—so to bed!

289

Thursday June 30 (Day of the lakes)

Slept late and soundly—woke at eight—dressed and to hotel for breakfast—women feeding deer and laughing before hotel—The lake mist-blue in morning light—so back to cabin, packed, put things in car—talked to waitress sitting in grass with deer nestling to her—pretty picture—good-bye to Keyes, and away about 10 o'clock—The lake marvellous in morning shadow and the Alpine sheerness of the granite peaks—so

291

dropping down to Belton where looked at Chalet and rooms and talk with dejected manager; and boys hunting for elk horns—so away and down to Flathead Lake along a pleasant lovely stream (McDonald Creek) and around the loveliness of Flathead Lake for next hour or so—a beautiful blue with the granite masses of the Continental divide rising on the other side

293

and cedar hills on the right—and lumber mills and trains of logs and much timber like Olympia again—so leave the lake at Polson and so down into the Missoula valley—the Rocky range away eastward and lower ridges to the west—the valley widening; the district of Flathead Indians, opened as late as 1910 for white settlement the river somewhere away to the right—told by a line of trees

295

but out of sight—so down to the junction at ? and decide on the road to the right by the bison range instead of Missoula, so along this road and by the bison camp and Flathead reservation, and pick up the stream again, this time a marvellous glorious viscous emerald green now known as Clark's Fork (of the Columbia River) and for 200 miles, to Newport (?)

297

on the Washington state line, along this stream which constantly enlarges and grows deeper—a lovely ride along a valley, the scenery often almost Appalachian (save for the darkness of the trees), the valley, in this pinery and this land of mighty sweeps surprisingly intimate and narrow now, very sparsely settled, but breaking out now and then into wealths and sweeps of green

299

fertility, the green glacial stream constantly being fed by others, drawing all the water from the hills into itself, being widened and thickened but muddied by the confluence of the Bitter Root River—a strange sight now—the left side of the river glacial green, the right side muddy brown, the country now most thickly forested with dark and lordly trees—

300

—and back at Thompson's Falls—the blistered little town (the Montana towns have more of a false-front, shack-like old West appearance than any other I have seen—and three little girls dancing in front of the place where we eat and the railway grade above and opposite, the N.P. station and the blistered houses; so away along the river again, and pick up a train and follow down it

298

and at last come upon the Pen D'Oreille Lake (in Idaho in the panhandle)—a rather big lake and a lovely one, swollen with rains and increased by flood—and along the lake and at last to Kootenai and big farms, well painted buildings, warm alfalfa and green fields, and so pick up the river (the Clark Fork again) now known as the Pen

296

D'Oreille, and further speculation on the route of Lewis and of Clark, whose ghosts have haunted us and this country since Three Forks and the upper reaches of the Missouri and so along the river until we cross it finally at Newport, and the river sweeping North toward Canada and the great loop and its final return with the mighty Columbia and we away for the last

294

40 or 50 miles into Spokane—the country already has a Pacific northwest look (I thought)—the dark trees, pines predominant, and some larches, and all greener there I thought (the whole journey today has been green and thick with forest, full of water) and so into Spokane in good time (at 6:45 Pacific time)

292

and to the Davenport Hotel and a bottle of Scotch and conversation, and C, M and a friend *downstairs to dinner, and presently I go down alone, and eat, and then upstairs and straighten accounts with Conway (the whole trip costing me less than $50.00)—and then down to send telegram to Chase bank and to Roundup place for beer, and so home a little after one to bed.*

290

—Up at 7:45—and dressed packed—downstairs to ***Friday July 1*** *breakfast with C and M in coffeeshop of Davenport—and two of their friends—and so talking and at last away at 9:50 and west from Spokane through country being more barren all the time and sweeps of wheat fields and desert and sage brush country—so to the turn off for Grand Coulee and mounting up and then down through a dry bend and the great walls, the basaltic walls*

288

of the Grand Coulee down, down, down and the tremendous size and glacial greenness of the Columbia river sweeping round the bend and the basal ramparts of the terrific dam, and the crews with red helmets working, so to the observation point and fidgeted and listened to a talk on the dimensions and purpose of the dam (so made to

hear another talk with a model—the power flumes
and the giant pumps the

286

giant figures—so down and across the bridge to
Mason City where the workers live—and as much
like the rude West as one can find now—and so
back and up again and by crews working,
gathered in red helmets and to the top of the
plateau, and now following out the route of the
Dry Coulee the cavernous basaltic walls and the
ancient and enormous bed—then

284

to the great basin of the Dry falls and then down
down down to the Coulees end and into the
dry sagebrush desert, and across this desert that
the dam will reclaim, and under burning skies,
and corroded desert—by it at great speed—and a
pause for lunch and on again and towards the
hot blue haze of hills and up and up the canyon
of a constantly rising

282

plateau, and the air cool now and the wind
beating so the car rocks and swerves like a toy
and down and down the gorge of the Yakimas

into the upper end of the Yakima valley at Ellenton then into the Yakima gorge and the dry hills again and up and around and along the narrow gorge above the rushing river and at last into Yakima where turning follow

280

back along the valley of the Naches and this too burgeoning with fruit and the dry hills closing in and into the Canyon Gorge again and the boiling river flowing past and trees now, and climbing climbing, and the forest darkness now of the Cascades—pine, hemlock, spruce, some fir—and up the American river again into blue black Cascades and forests night dark now, and mist gathering

278

and clouds overhead and mists deepening and thickening and blowing ice sheets of spume through the Chinook Pass, and through the pass and down and fog and mist more thick than leaden fog, and down the road into the valley past the rangers gate and up again and the milk white of the Glacier creek and around and up climbing hard now and all lost vaguely

274

in mist and around again and the great white bowl masses of Ranier descried and mist blowing in in floods of spume and up and up to timber line and to the Sunrise Lodge and light playing marvellously, and blue cerulean, struggling to break through, and the glaciers level to the eye and visible but the great mountain massif and the peak obscured—so over the snow still 4 to six feet deep to our cabins—then to dinner

272

at the Lodge—a state of unfurnishment yet, and the cold menace and terror of the mountain, the gigantic fume flames of bright mist sweeping by below us, above us, and around the mighty mass —then with the Ranger to the administration office to see his collection of rocks, flowers, and models, then to the cabin where Ranger built a fire, and talking with M about the trip—and very tired, and presently to bed.

276

the vast grey green of the plains—in the land-mouldings a silken sheen

The blue blazing sky, the clouds cumulous, crested, crowded against infinity, packed with immeasurable light.

And the Rockies half shrouded into both light and cloud—the magic of the sky marvellous

The faery green of the glacial lakes

270

Lay late, until 8:20—and C came in to build the fire, and in both of us quiet greetings, a feeling that our trip was almost done, and in me a sense of the tremendous kindness and decency and humanity of the man. He said: "Tom, look at the mountain!" I got up and looked; it was immense and terrific and near and cloud still clung to the Great

Saturday July 2

268

Cloudmaker at the side like a great filament of ectoplasm. C told me to sleep as long as I wanted, and went out but presently I got up and the room warm now and a brisk fire going in the stove and a basin of water and dressed and shaved, and walked over the packed and dirty snow to the Lodge, where joined C and Caderon at breakfast—and Caderon

266

a nice boy, doing his level best for us in everything, solicitous and good—the long face and teeth and loving agreeability of the Y.M.C.A.

and Sunday School boy—he spoke frequently of his Sunday School Class—So M joined us, refreshed from sleep, and the Ranger and another Ranger, and so out to take pictures and to look at the Mountain—and the sun out now, the

264

mist ocean still below us—but the great mass of Rainer clearly defined now, save for the white sky-backwall—and the great mass faced up squarely and all its perilous overwhelming majesty, and with its tremendous shoulders, the long terrific sweeps of its hackling ridges, we stood trying to get its scale, and this

262

impossible because there was nothing but Mountain—a universe of mountain, a continent of mountain—and nothing else but mountain itself to compare mountain to. On this trip C's great love and knowledge of mountains has revealed itself—upon the summit of the pass at the Continental divide in Glacier the way he pointed out the little trees, the affection and reverence with which he spoke of them—the signs by which the

260

trees of timber-line could be observed and noted
the Cloudiness at the Base etc—the little
mountain flowers—now the astounding revelation
that he had climbed Hood 225 times and Ranier
40—the quiet way he told of accidents and
rescues—of the ice so hard that the axe bounds
off and "ruins a man for life"—of the crevasse—
of the man who fell and

258

drove his Alpine stock through him and of how
he got him out but didn't dare touch the Alpine
stock, and of how they got the man down off the
mountain and of how "he lived several hours.
He was conscious."—and of another young man
that he had rescued two or three years before and
of how he could see him lying on a ledge in the
crevasse

256

and how his heart sank for he saw the broken
axe and Alpine stock and was "afraid it had
gone through him too"—but how he was "all
right except that he was all cut up" and I got
the rope about him and we got him out and
sewed him up with a darning needle and ordinary
thread, and he's as good today as he ever was"—
and C. laughed—Made

254

farewells and away by 11:30 or so and down the mountain into the sea of cold fog and mist again —the great forests now—dropping below the mists the enormous forest darkness of the Douglas firs, the towering trunks of the terrific trees, the dense fervid darkness of the undergrowth—then blasted woods, denuded hills and acres of stumps and snow, and then the lowlands—a casual margin land at

252

first of farms and woods and natural growth and nondescript houses, barns, etc—curiously ragged, casual, and unkept looking after the irrigated lands, then out and down into the valley, and the level, farms, the fruit trees, and the towns, and so Tacoma and so out along the broad four-wayed Pacific Highway towards Olympia, and the four

250

lanes already busy with their traffic of the Fourth and the strings of market stores, hot dog stands, filling stations, taverns, etc. so down into the crowded streets of Olympia choked with great tides of traffic for the Fourth, the sidewalks crowded with throngs of people—farmers, seamen, lumberjacks in town for the Fourth—so parked the car and to Cranes famous seafood Restaurant

248

for lunch, and ate a shrimp cocktail of the tiny Puget shrimps, and then a delicious pan roast of the small but succulent Puget Sound oysters, the whole cooked in with crab meat in a delicious pungent sauce and spread on toast so eaten, most delicious—and so our farewells new addresses, final instructions—the casuallike wordiness of men with some sadness in their

246

heart avoiding farewells—and C, still avoiding it (how like my brother!) is going to run me up to see the Capitol and we see it, and still avoiding it, back to see the old State Capitol, and we see it—and they give me the map and old Tour Book we have worn black, and write their names in it—and at last, farewell—and they are gone, and

244

a curiously hollow feeling in me as I stand there in the streets of Olympia and watch the white Ford flash away—

So stay an hour or so and watch the town, and miss one bus and catch another at 4:35, and to

Seattle, the great bus keeping to the inner line at good speed, the magnificent four-ply highway filled with the flashing traffic of

242

the holiday, the country undulant in long sweeps between the dark and ragged lines of Douglas fir —the temporary congestion of Tacoma, and the bus halt there—then on our way again on the great highway and presently the outskirts of Seattle, scattered houses, open country, the Arms of Puget Sound—blue-black, misty and exciting under the grey

240

skies, and then the great train yards, flying field, viaducts—the settlements upon the hills, then the Railway stations and the full town, the downtown section, "Big House", the crowded streets, the long pull up the slope of Second Avenue, the bus station, a taxi, the hotel, telegrams there from Nowell and Ed that

238

(*End of the Trip*)

make me very happy, money from the bank, a bottle of Scotch liquor, a midnight meal at Rippes —and, the trip over now, to bed!

150

	Square Mileages	
Oregon	*96,690*	
California	*155,652*	
Arizona	*113,956*	
Utah	*83,990*	(*about 30% of*
Idaho	*84,000*	*entire national area*)
Wyoming	?	
Montana	*146,997*	
Washington	*69,127*	
	750,412	
	100,000 (?)	

4

Spokane, Friday June 31

And the notes, the impressions

The little slaughtered wild things in the road—in Oregon, in California, across the desert, going up—through Utah, in Idaho, Wyoming, and Montana—the little crushed carcasses of the gophers, chipmunks, jackrabbits, birds—in the hot bright western light the black crows picking at some furry mangled little carcass on the hot road—rises and flaps slowly vauntingly away as the car approaches

6

In that lively rolling of the White Ford through Montana, in full afternoon-heat and the brightness of the sun of the transcontinental freight of the N.P. blasting towards us up the grade, the interminable freight cars climbing past and suddenly—the tops of the great train lined with clusters of hoboes—a hundred of them—some sprawled out, sitting, others erect, some stretched out on their backs

8

lazily inviting the luminous American weather, and the mountain ranges all around, the glacial green of the Clark's Fork just beyond—and the 'bos roll past across America silently regarding us—the pity, terror, strangeness, and magnificence of it all.

Notes

These few notes are set here rather than as footnotes to avoid interrupting the flow of Wolfe's writing. Italic type and the irregular length of line are used in the hope that they may suggest, at least a little, his quick-running script.

The boldface arabic figures are facsimiles of the numbers on the pages of the ledger in which he wrote the *Journal.*

3. *Bent* should, of course, be Bend, as it is below on the same page.

8. The printing of page 8 interrupts page 7, because to have it follow 7, as 8 would normally, would disturb the flow of Wolfe's sentence from 7 to 9.

19. *a brief halt at* ———. The omission is Wolfe's.

29. *the turn at* ———. The omission is Wolfe's; probably Merced.

46. Set to follow 47 so as not to break the flow of thought from 45 to 47 (probably the order of Wolfe's writing it, anyway).

58. Another afterthought, apparently, and another departure from right-hand sequence.

71. *Big Gorgooby*, it is very evident, is Wolfe's name for the Grand Canyon.

73. *rudeeleven.* Of this word we are not absolutely certain.

77. *unvital.* Another uncertain word.

155. *lemon hay*. The word *lemon* is by no means certain.

218. *the big*   *of grain elevators*. This space in the ledger is filled with Wolfe's rough line drawing representing a grain elevator. The editors agreed to change the word *road* to *vast* in the second printing. See reproduction of page 218.

226. The question mark is Wolfe's; probably Jenny Lake.

238. Here Wolfe drew a line. See note 298.

295. *junction at ?* The question mark is Wolfe's. The word probably is Ravalli, which is the town at junction of Alt. 10 and 93.

295. Newport (?) This question mark, also, is Wolfe's. The word probably is Idaho. Newport is on the Idaho-Washington line and Alt. Route 10 passes through the panhandle of Idaho from Montana to Washington. (It is approximately 200 miles from Polson to Newport.)

300. *back at Thompson's Falls.* Here Wolfe goes back in recollection to the trip he had made over Alt. 10 before he entered the Idaho panhandle.

298. Here Wolfe starts the business of writing backwards in the notebook, of writing on the left-hand pages in unbroken sequence until he reaches p. 238, where he writes below the line drawn (see note 238) the end of his account of the trip.

238. (*End of the Trip*) See p. vii, viii of this book for explanation of pages 150, 4, 6, 8 which follow.

Square Mileage

Oregon	96,690
California	155,652
Arizona	113,956
Utah	83,990
Idaho	84,000
Wyoming	?
Montana	146,997
Washington	69,127
	750417 (?)
	+ 100 000

(abt 30% of entire national area)